THE
DOOM
LOOP!

*Straight Talk about Job Frustration, Boredom,
Career Crises and Tactical Career Decisions
from the Doom Loop Creator*

CHARLES CRANSTON JETT

DENVER, COLORADO

The DOOM LOOP!
. . . .Straight Talk about Job Frustration, Boredom, Career Crises and Tactical Career Decisions from the Doom Loop Creator.

Outskirts Press, Inc.
http://www.outskirtspress.com

Paperback ISBN: 978-1-4787-4304-0
Hardback ISBN: 978-1-4787-4523-5

Library of Congress Control Number: 2014915880

Outskirts Press and the "OP" logo are trademarks belonging to Outskirts Press, Inc.

PRINTED IN THE UNITED STATES OF AMERICA

WHAT PEOPLE ARE SAYING
ABOUT *THE DOOM LOOP*

I was first introduced to Charlie Jett's Doom Loop when I was having my own career crisis in my early thirties. The model made an instant and lasting impression on me for its simplicity, accuracy and applicability. Since my first exposure to the Doom Loop, I have shared it with hundreds of leaders and senior executives through my work and am invariably met with the same instant recognition and understanding. I'm a huge fan of simple models that work and the Doom Loop is at the top of my list. It is useful, memorable and a phenomenal tool to quickly understand how to increase engagement, job satisfaction and productivity. - *Glaine Roberts-McCabe, President; The Executive Roundtable Inc.; Toronto, Canada*

I have been using the "Doom Loop" ever since Charlie Jett introduced me to this elegant career management tool over 30 years ago to coach students, MBA graduates, Consulting Partners and countless others about career opportunities. It works! My approach is that most high potential employees and executives need a "new mountain to climb" every 2-3 years within the same company, outside the company, or even a different country and culture. The career capstone approach works and helps executives sharpen their skill sets in preparation for broader responsibilities. This approach, along with the guidance of the Doom Loop, is an excellent example of how to grow and reach a capstone of a true "global executive." Congratulations, Charlie, on an excellent book. It's a "must read." - *Roger Nelson, Retired Deputy Chairman, Ernst & Young LLC*

I was first introduced to Charlie Jett's Doom Loop in the 1980s and was immediately struck by how simple yet profound it was. Over the past 20 years, I have made hundreds of presentations on careers and have always presented the Doom Loop concept. And, no surprise to me, it is one of the most remembered discussion points by audience members. People will contact me years later and say "I need your help...I remember you talking about a Doom Loop and I'm in it! HELP!" - *John R. Bertrand, Ph.D.; Marshall School of Business; University of Southern California*

ACKNOWLEDGEMENTS

There are many who contributed ideas and encouragement to the creation of the Doom Loop and I would like to acknowledge their contribution and generously thank them. First, to "Uncle Charlie" at the Naval Academy who taught us, "You can do anything you set your mind to do!" to Dr. Barrie S. Greiff of the Harvard Business School whose idea it was to make a simple static matrix a dynamic tool; to my friends, Fred Wackerle, Roger Nelson, and Glaine Roberts-McCabe for their thoughtful comments about the manuscript; to the late Dr. Dory Hollander who popularized the Doom Loop in the 1990's; to my two boys, Charlie and Christopher, who put up with their dad's travel and work as they plowed through school; to my loving wife, Dr. Nancy Church, who pushed me forward with constant encouragement to just "get it done;" to George Berlin for his creative graphics and funny movie on the website; and finally, to the outstanding team at Outskirts Press - Terri for her initial guidance, Joan for her peerless editing, and Dana for her publication savvy. Together you made the publication process a pleasure. Well done!

TABLE OF CONTENTS

INTRODUCTION

The news certainly caused me to stand up and take notice. A recent Gallup poll reported that *"Seventy-one percent of American workers are 'not engaged' or are 'actively disengaged' in their work, meaning they are emotionally disconnected from their workplaces and are less likely to be productive. That leaves nearly one-third of American workers who are 'engaged,' or involved in and enthusiastic about their work and contributing to their organizations in a positive manner."*

Could it be, I thought, that over two-thirds of American workers are *"doomed"*?

That is "Doom Loop Language," and the purpose of this book is to provide some straight talk about what the Doom Loop is and what it does.

Many years have passed since I created the Doom Loop back in the late 1970s. Since that time, it has been described as a disarmingly simple but very potent way to explain a lot very quickly. Many others, including me, have spent time in a variety of settings (mostly over a cocktail) generally talking to others about where their careers are on the Doom Loop and developing simple tactical decisions about how to deal with it.

It is a fact that others and I have used this career management tool on countless occasions to counsel individuals informally, so my approach to this book will be as though I am having a personal conversation with YOU. Therefore, I will not refer to "an individual," or "he/she," etc., *but will speak directly to you.*

Workplace boredom has a distinct effect on worker productivity. This should ring bells in the minds of managers and lead to a more open dialog with workers — after all, executives strive to achieve a high degree of productivity in their organizations. It seems logical that managers would spend time and effort to reduce the level of boredom in their workforce. They should be aware of the natural consequences of the Doom Loop. If what the Gallup organization reports is true, there are a lot of other people who might benefit from its wisdom.

The Doom Loop is not something to be afraid of; in fact, it should be considered a useful friend. The Doom Loop really isn't a "loop" at all, but a catchy name.

The purpose of this book is to provide a simple and quick description of this effective little tool so that you might be able to use it yourself or describe it to others right away. In doing so, you must understand that the Doom Loop is not perfect and should not be considered a highly accurate tool. Its use is limited in that it considers only two variables: preference and performance. There are many other variables that enter into career and personal equations, so whenever one considers using the Doom Loop, consider it a rough guide, not a precision measuring instrument. There are various interpretations of the Doom Loop that have been circulated over the years, and those that claim that the tool can very accurately measure where you are in any stage of your career are simply wrong. Keep this in mind as you read about, describe, or use the Doom Loop.

The Doom Loop is not hard to understand; in fact, it is clearly intuitive and very easy to remember. That is why this book is rather short: you don't need to plow through a lot of rhetoric to understand and use such a simple and intuitive concept. You also do not need to enroll in all-day workshops or seminars and conduct exercises to position yourself exactly somewhere in the Doom Loop matrix. That is a waste of time. Accordingly, this book should be a "quick read" to enable you to quickly grasp the concept and apply it to yourself, or use it to counsel others.

My efforts to get the word out about the Doom Loop included not only the many speeches and presentations I was giving at the time, but a video as well. In 1987 Northwestern University sponsored a video about career management in which I described the Doom Loop as well as the Critical Skills. You can watch that video at the following link: http://thedoomloopblog. com/the-movie/ It was intended primarily for MBA students.

It is a mistake to think of the Doom Loop as applying only to MBA students or for those individuals who aspire to upper-level management and are frantically trying to climb the corporate ladder. In fact, you may be among the many individuals in the American workforce who are not trying to climb that ladder, but are experiencing frustration and boredom on the job, and this book is definitely intended for you!

As a matter of appreciation, I would like to pay tribute and thanks to the late Dr. Dory Hollander, to whom I introduced the Doom Loop at the national convention of the American Psychological Association (APA) back in the mid-1980s. She and I made several presentations together in various venues — including one presentation to the national convention of the APA. Dr. Hollander was instrumental in popularizing the Doom Loop through a book called *The Doom Loop System*, which I outlined for her. While I commend her for her efforts and thank her for being honest in attributing the creation of the Doom Loop to me in the introduction and in Chapter One of the book, I feel that the book attempted to take the Doom Loop much too seriously and make it something that, quite frankly, it is not. Others have written about it as well. Some have been thoughtful enough to give attribution — and some have not. Their thoughts are included in Chapter Twelve.

Now it is time to reintroduce the Doom Loop to you in a simple way so that many people — including yourself, as well as perhaps 71 % of the American workforce who are apparently bored and frustrated in their jobs — can benefit from its wise counsel! I am writing this book purely from memory without consultation from any resource, and my goal is to equip you with an understanding of the mechanics of the Doom Loop without your having to attend some long and boring seminar or workshop. *This should ensure that the Doom Loop is described for you exactly as it was originally intended to be.*

The organization of this book is simple. I will present a short history of the Doom Loop, describe it in detail, and then show its application for seven crises that you will most likely encounter during the course of your career. I will try to keep the descriptions brief and simple, and will present a few case studies and/or examples of how the tool was used in each of the different career crises, where appropriate. I will not provide any checklists, exercises, or monotonous descriptions of tertiary uses of the Doom Loop, simply because I think those uses are pure nonsense. The Doom Loop is intended to be simple, intuitive, and one of the many guides you might use in making *tactical* career decisions from time to time. It is not a "strategic career tool" or any sort of "system" — those are reserved for skill building and mastering Critical Skills as described in detail in my book, *WANTED: Eight Critical Skills You Need To Succeed. Most important — it is NOT a complete "career management system" and should never be or ever have been considered in that context.*

So let us begin the journey!

Chapter One
HISTORY OF THE DOOM LOOP

It didn't come as a blinding flash, at least not like that allegedly experienced by Paul on his way to Damascus. But it was an epiphany of sorts — one of those "Aha!" moments when I felt that I had stumbled upon something simple that had practical value.

It was the recruiting season for MBAs in the late 1970s and I was interviewing Harvard Business School candidates for management consulting with the firm of Booz Allen. The student whom I was interviewing was smart, but really didn't have the kind of qualifications that we were looking for. He was very nice and rather sensitive, so I decided to use some management consulting tactics to demonstrate why the consulting profession might not be right for him.

We were in Boston, so my first thought was of the Boston Consulting Group (BCG) which was quite well-known for its use of 2 x 2 matrices to describe business opportunities. Therefore, I thought that a 2 x 2 matrix might be appropriate in discussing the possibility of his working in the consulting field.

A cocktail napkin was handy and I drew a matrix that had "good at" and "not good at" on the left (ordinate), and "like" and "don't like" on the top (abscissa). Using two variables of what someone might experience in a job seemed to make sense. Then I labeled each quadrant of the matrix as "Q1, Q2, Q3, and Q4."

	LIKE	DON'T LIKE
GOOD AT	Happy Satisfied Q2	Frustrated Bored Q3
NOT GOOD AT	Q1 Challenged Motivated	Q4 Unhappy Miserable

The next step was to show him how he would feel when in the various quadrants.

- If he is "not good at" something but "likes" it, he would be in Quadrant 1 (Q1). There he would have feelings of being anxious, challenged, motivated, and perhaps a bit uptight.

- If he is "good at" something and "likes" it, he would be in Quadrant 2 (Q2). There he would have feelings of happiness and satisfaction.

- If he is "good at" something but "doesn't like" it, he would be in Quadrant 3 (Q3) and would have feelings of frustration and boredom.
- Finally, if he is "not good at" something and "doesn't like" it, he would be in Quadrant 4 (Q4) and would essentially be unhappy and miserable.

The student looked at the matrix and immediately concluded that were he to enter the management consulting field, he would start somewhere in Q4 — unhappy and miserable. He then said that he appreciated my taking the time to interview him, but that he had concluded that the field was not for him, thanked me for my time, and left the interview room.

I began to stare at the matrix; it made sense! It was simple!

Later on, I presented the matrix to the Harvard Business School psychiatrist, Dr. Barrie S. Greiff. He liked the concept and then made an interesting comment: "It would be interesting to see what happens over time — as an individual progressed in a job."

That's all he said. And another *"Aha!"* came to me.

I decided to look at what might happen when an individual takes a job and gains competence in the various things he/she might be responsible for doing.

It is important to understand here that the matrix tracks two things:

- If a person likes or doesn't like something (preferences); and

- If a person is not good at or good at the same things (performance).

There are obviously many other variables — some relevant and some irrelevant — that enter into one's feelings in a job, such as:

- Does the person like the business?
- Does the person like the people in his/her organization?
- Does the person like the town in which he/she is residing?
- Does the person like chocolate ice cream? Etc.

You can think of hundreds of things that you might like or dislike, but for the purposes of this analysis, those things can be held constant or simply ignored. This is very similar to what an engineer or mathematician might do to analyze a problem: hold some variables constant while performing analyses on others over time. In a sense, this is an application of "partial differential equations," but in this case, the variables and measurements are qualitative rather than quantitative.

I then thought of a scenario where you might take a new job. When you take that job and are aware of the kinds of things that you must do on the job, obviously there will be some things that you like and dislike (most would be in the "like" category, or you would probably not be considering the job), and some would be in the "good at" and "not good" at category. I ignored for the moment all of the other variables in the job evaluation equation.

If you plot the cluster of these two variables on the 2 x 2 matrix, it would appear as follows:

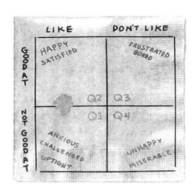

Given that all other variables are being held constant or ignored for the moment, you would have feelings of happiness and satisfaction in some parts of the job, but you would also have feelings of being challenged, motivated, anxious, and perhaps would be a bit uptight.

This is not bad at all! Being "not good at" something is not bad — *provided that you have an ability to learn!* In fact, taking a job where there are things to learn and motivate you is a good thing. It makes you want to learn, to practice and master those things you are supposed to be doing, and keeps you motivated! For simplicity's sake, let us call the time you are looking at this "T1."

I then thought about what would happen as time progresses and you are still in the same job but have the opportunity to "get good at" some of those things that were initially challenging. If you plot the cluster at a later time, call it "T2," the cluster would appear as follows:

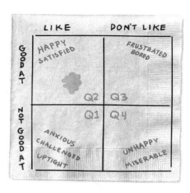

The cluster would have moved up from Q1 into Q2 and you would be having feelings of being happy and satisfied on the job, mainly because you would have "gotten good at" those things that were previously challenging.

As time passes by, however, and you stay in the same job, doing the tasks over and over again, at this later time, "T3," the cluster will move upward and to the right as follows:

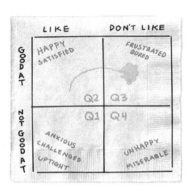

In Q3, feelings of frustration and boredom set in. You are stuck in a job doing the same old things. Being in Q3 can be a bit dangerous for you if you are trying to manage your career because it can make you vulnerable to a lot of things — such as making wrong decisions by changing jobs, etc. These vulnerabilities will be discussed in the chapters describing the various career crises.

As time wears on and you are still in the same job doing the same thing, the frustration and boredom might lead to your not staying current with changing technology or other changes in the workplace that do not change what you are doing. This can lead to your performance starting to suffer and the cluster, if plotted at this time, T4, would start to move downward as follows:

 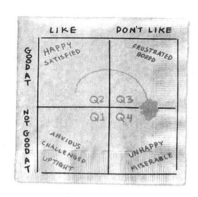

Obviously Q4 is not a quadrant in which anyone would enjoy finding him/herself. Being unhappy and miserable in a job is no fun.

The actual track of the cluster that one plots during the course of a job is what, in the late 1970s, I initially called the Doom Loop. While it really is not a loop per se, the name is catchy and easy to remember. *So it is a Doom Loop!* Graphically it appears as follows:

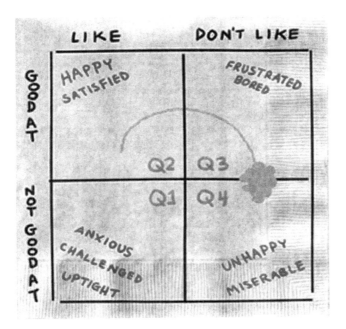

Here is the key point:

> **Any job that you have ever had, have, or ever will have
> has a Doom Loop associated with it so long as the job
> and the requisite tasks regarding that job do not change
> over time. This is true, of course, providing that you
> have the capacity to learn — and are capable of having
> feelings.**

There are things that you can do to manage the Doom Loop
for yourself, and actually *predict* where you might be headed
at different times in your career. These will be described in the
various chapters on career crises.

An interesting point about the Doom Loop curve that needs definition is the point at the maximum top of the curve where, for you mathematicians, the slope of the curve is zero. That point is shown as follows:

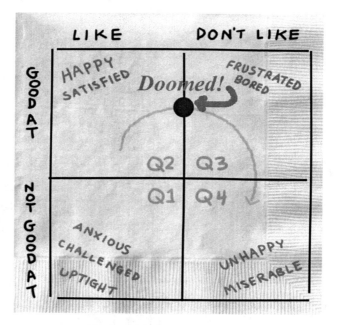

Whenever you are in a job where the tasks do not change and you reach the top of the curve, you are *"doomed." This term is important to remember.*

Don't worry, though. You're not really "doomed" in a classical sense — just in the context of this fun little career management tool.

The nice thing is that you can actually do something about it!

First, however, let's take a look at seven career crises.

The Seven Career Crises

There are seven career crises that nearly everyone who is working, has worked before, or ever will work is bound to face. Each of these crises will be discussed in subsequent chapters of this book. The crises are as follows:

- The First Job
- First Job Disappointment
- Happy Below Capstone, but Doomed
- Doomed Before Capstone
- Fired
- Doomed at Capstone
- Retirement

With the exception of the first two career crises — the first job and first job disappointment — each of the career crises may be examined with respect to the Doom Loop. All seven of the career crises are predictable.

So let's get started!

Chapter Two

THE SKILL MOSAIC

Webster's dictionary defines *skill* as *"the ability to do something that comes from training, experience, or practice."* This is the definition that I use: not some trait or characteristic that someone might have, but actually something that individual learns through training, experience, or practice.

There are many different kinds of skills. Whether they are relevant within a particular context is entirely dependent upon individual circumstances. For example, what are the kinds of skills needed by:

- A physician
- A lawyer
- A business executive
- An airline pilot
- A professional athlete
- A citizen in a democratic society
- A book editor
- Etc.

Clearly the skill sets for such roles are different. In fact, within each generalized set of roles there is a wide variety of subsets. For example, a physician might be a general practitioner, a surgeon, a dermatologist, an obstetrician/gynecologist, a neurologist, etc. While there are overlapping skills within each of these medical specialties, the total skill set is different for each. This is the same for the other roles listed.

My first exposure to and focus on skill sets was in the corporate world. As a management consultant, I dealt with individuals who held different corporate management positions, such as Chief Executive Officer, Vice President — Finance, Vice President — Marketing, Corporate Treasurer, Vice President — Human Resources, and the like. Each of these positions had different skill sets as well.

One of the roles I filled was to be a spokesperson at many of the nation's top business schools at the MBA level: Harvard, Stanford, Wharton, Northwestern, Michigan, University of Chicago, etc. I managed the corporate recruiting program for a major management consulting firm and often was required to speak in front of large audiences of bright-eyed and eager MBA students, all wanting to get ahead in the corporate world.

While my lectures to these groups initially were to promote our consulting firm and to encourage students to interview with us, I was later invited to these schools to give talks to larger groups of students about a strategy for *how to get ahead in the corporate world*. The challenge was to give them advice and a simple strategy to progress up the ladder in the field of their choosing and in a wide variety of businesses. Nearly all if not all of the students had a goal to eventually become a Chief Executive Officer (CEO).

I knew the answer to the question of how to advance in a corporate environment was to learn and demonstrate mastery of skills in doing a job. I also knew that in order to gain access to top management, there was a threshold level of management — I called it a *first career capstone position* — a position through which an individual **must** pass in order to advance to upper-level management. Such first career capstone positions included those in which the individual is actually in charge of some function or group . . . such as a vice president — finance, or a vice president — marketing, or perhaps a first-level partner in a management consulting, accounting, or law firm.

Accordingly I used a graphic approach and presented to them a *skill field*, which was intended to display the *skill mosaic* that the individual builds during his/her career on the way to a first career capstone position. This skill field appears as follows:

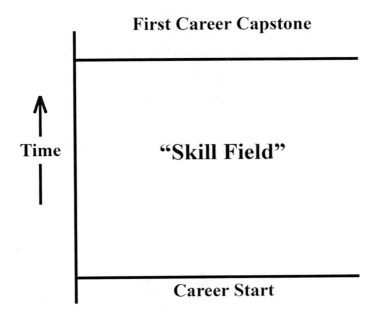

My intent was to show the first career capstone positions at the top of the graphic and then show, over time, the strategic building of a skill mosaic that would qualify an individual to be promoted to such a position. Time progressed upward on the left and when an individual took a job with the organization following graduation, he/she would start at the bottom at *Career Start.*

An example of the skill mosaic for a vice president — finance is as follows:

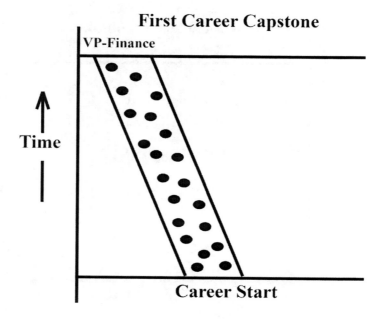

First Career Capstone

The dots represent skills mastered in this particular mosaic for the VP — finance.

For a vice president — marketing, the skill mosaic would look as follows, again with the dots representing skills associated with that mosaic:

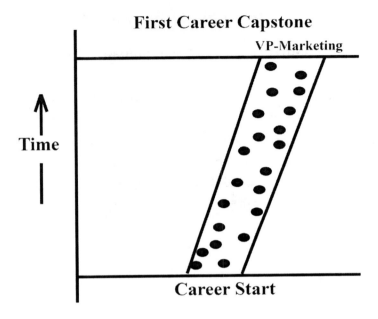

First Career Capstone

VP-Marketing

Time

Career Start

Clearly the skill mosaics for the two positions are different. The skills needed to become a VP — finance are specific to that position, as are the skills of a VP — marketing. As an example of the skills contained in a skill mosaic, one needs only to go to The Occupational Information Network (O*NET), which is a free online database that contains hundreds of occupational definitions to help students, job seekers, businesses, and work-force development professionals to understand today's world of work in the United States. http://www.onetcenter.org/ The amount of detail provided in O*Net job descriptions is actually more than one needs to adequately describe a job; however, for demonstration purposes, a summary description of a typical vice president — marketing first career capstone position taken directly from O*Net is as follows:

Vice President — Marketing

The vice president — marketing will plan, direct, or coordinate marketing policies and programs, such as determining the demand for products and services offered by the company and its competitors, and identify potential customers. He/she will develop pricing strategies with the goal of maximizing the firm's profits or share of the market while ensuring the firm's customers are satisfied. He/she will oversee product development or monitor trends that indicate the need for new products and services.

Responsibilities:

- Formulate, direct, and coordinate marketing activities and policies to promote products and services, working with advertising and promotion managers.

- Identify, develop, or evaluate marketing strategy, based on knowledge of establishment objectives, market characteristics, and cost and markup factors.

- Direct the hiring, training, or performance evaluations of marketing or sales staff and oversee their daily activities.

- Evaluate the financial aspects of product development, such as budgets, expenditures, research and development appropriations, or return-on-investment and profit-loss projections.

- Develop pricing strategies, balancing firm objectives and customer satisfaction.

- Compile lists describing product or service offerings.

- Initiate market research studies or analyze their findings.

- Use sales forecasting or strategic planning to ensure the sale and profitability of products, lines, or services, analyzing business developments and monitoring market trends.

- Coordinate or participate in promotional activities or trade shows, working with developers, advertisers, or production managers, to market products or services.

- Consult with buying personnel to gain advice regarding the types of products or services expected to be in demand.

My point to the students was that if they wanted to rise to the level of top management, they should adopt a strategy to target a particular first career capstone position such as the vice president — marketing, and concentrate on building a mosaic that, in their particular organization, would qualify them for that position.

I made the additional point that in the world of the executive recruiter, the process is to build not only a position description for one of the capstone positions, but also to articulate the skills that are necessary to have in order to be a qualified candidate for the job. Similarly, organizations that promote from within should ensure that any individual who might be in line for such a position has the skill mosaic pertinent to that particular position.

The use of a skill mosaic depends on who is using it. Students and those working their way up the career ladder should think of strategically building their mosaic into some clearly recognizable "picture" of a target first career capstone position. This picture or mosaic has to make sense and contain demonstrated evidence of skill achievement and mastery in order for an individual to be promoted.

The executive recruiter, however, looks at the mosaic from a different viewpoint. Graphically, the executive recruiter is looking for a clear mosaic of skills that paints a picture of the kind of position for which the search is being conducted. Once a candidate who has a mosaic that closely matches is found, the process of candidate evaluation can begin.

The issue of what actually qualifies a candidate for a position is a different matter. Recruiters generally look for candidates who have mastered the skills in the mosaic contained in the position specification. Logically, one would assume, the candidate who is "good at" most of the skills in the mosaic is the best candidate — *but I don't agree with this at all, and I explain this situation in a later chapter.*

Then I went on to show to the students the overlap of the two different positions, demonstrating that for these particular positions, there are skills that are common to both. This is shown as follows:

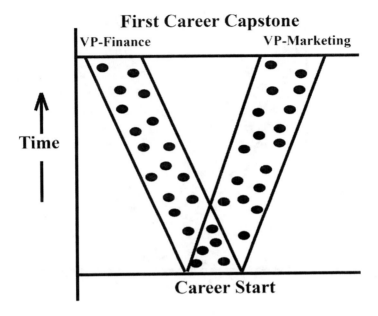

I pointed out that the skills common to each position are skills that they **must** master no matter what position they are targeting. These are the skills I defined as Critical Skills, and are shown as follows:

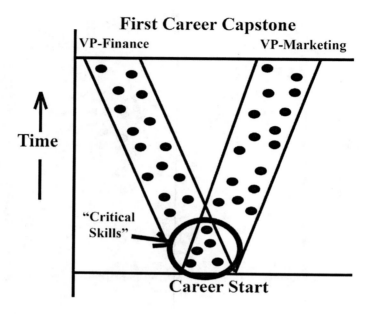

First Career Capstone

The intent of this book is not to provide an in-depth discussion of the Critical Skills; that task is reserved for my book *Wanted: Eight Critical Skills You Need to Succeed!* However, there are eight Critical Skills, and they are defined as follows, in order of priority.

Communication

The ability to get ideas out of your head and into the heads of others; the ability to get ideas out of someone else's head and into your own — all through the process of reading, writing, listening, and speaking.

Production

The Production Skill is often referred to as "making it happen." Simply put, it is the ability to convert an idea into reality . . . to convert a concept or idea into a product.

Information

The Information Skill is the ability to gather and sort relevant information pertaining to a particular problem to be solved or issue to be resolved. The skill also implies that the information gathered and sorted is judged or proved to be true.

Analysis

The Analysis Skill is the process of developing findings from facts, conclusions from findings, and well-reasoned recommendations from conclusions.

It is best described by $P \rightarrow Q$, or "P" implies "Q." This is logic in its simplest form — a syllogism: a logical argument that uses deductive reasoning to arrive at a conclusion based on one or more hypotheses that are or are assumed to be true. If the hypothesis (P) is true, then deductive reasoning can arrive at a conclusion (Q) that will be true. If the hypothesis (P) is not true, then even the best deductive reasoning will arrive at a conclusion that may or may not be true. One gathers information and facts which are tested for truth, derives findings from the facts (what the facts mean), and from the findings draws one or more conclusions.

Interpersonal

The Interpersonal Skill is not a skill that enables you to win friends.

Rather, it is a skill that is best described by how others view you after you have worked with them on the job or in some sort of project.

It is more of a teamwork skill.

It is NOT a political skill.

If you have the Interpersonal Skill, then after you have worked with others, you have left them with the feeling that you have contributed value to the effort.

Technology

The Technology Skill does **not** mean that you should be good at designing electronic circuit boards or anything that even resembles technical design or expertise.

Instead, the Technology Skill is simply an ability to **select** the appropriate technology that is most efficient and useful to accomplish a specific task.

Time Management

The Time Management Skill enables an individual to determine what tasks are most important and how to devote the appropriate amount of time to accomplish those tasks to a high level of quality.

Another way to look at the skill is this: You go to work in the morning and you know you have 10 things to do. Four of those things are critical . . . but **you** have to figure out which four of the ten are in that category. Then you have to do the best you can on the rest.

Continuous Education

The Continuous Education Skill is simply the ability to constantly learn new techniques, master changing technologies, keep up with changes in an industry, and the like. It recognizes that our world is changing rapidly through technology and other advances, and we need training and continuous learning to keep current in our fields.

The entire set of eight Critical Skills may be defined as *"the skills that an individual needs to master in order to advance in any career."*

- The Critical Skills do not replace content knowledge.
- The most important features of the Critical Skills are that they are relevant, and easy to understand and remember.
- The Critical Skills set is timeless.
- The quality of this set of Critical Skills is high.
- The Critical Skills cut across functional lines.

- The Critical Skills cut across industry lines.

- Each of the Critical Skills is a learned skill. Understanding and mastery of each of the Critical Skills improves with practice.

- The Critical Skills are necessary to advance in a career.

- Critical Skills are hard to teach.

- Assessing the level of mastery of the Critical Skills is difficult.

- A wide variety of training programs are available to teach the Critical Skills.

- Critical Skills are important in government — especially in a democratic society.

- Businesses can apply the Critical Skills in a variety of ways.

A fundamental principle in strategic career management using a career mosaic is as follows:

No matter what career you might embark upon, concentrate early on learning and mastering the Critical Skills!

Skills and Competencies

There is widespread confusion about what skills and competencies are, and there is no accepted protocol regarding appropriate categorization. Accordingly, in this book I am providing my own definitions of skills and competencies in a simple and hopefully understandable manner. The intent of the simplicity is to enhance understanding of how skills may be determined, assessed, and used in such practices as education, employee assessment, training, and recruiting.

Technically, the words skill and competency have essentially the same meaning: each represents an ability to do something well, successfully, or efficiently. Realistically in the context of today's world, they are not quite the same, particularly when referring to core competencies. We'll look first at skills.

Skills

We have already discussed the Critical Skills.

- The ability to communicate (Communications);
- Make things happen (Production);
- Gather and process information (Information);
- Analyze the information (Analysis);
- Work effectively as a member of a team (Interpersonal);
- Select the appropriate technology to solve a problem (Technology);
- Set priorities and manage time (Time Management); and
- Continuous Education, which cuts across all industries and functional areas.

Competencies

Core competencies, on the other hand, are very specific and can be dynamic. A core competency is generally defined as a unique capability or advantage that distinguishes an enterprise from its competitors. The term originated in a 1990 Harvard Business Review article authored by C.K. Prahalad and Gary Hamel. Core competencies define the things that a company is particularly "good at" and things that competitors would have difficulty in replicating.

Highly successful companies such as Apple and NIKE certainly know and have established Core Competencies relating to their traditional businesses, but these companies also have recognized and have demonstrated that business models change, and a company needs to periodically redefine or augment its stable of Core Competencies. NIKE, for example, is not only good at making and selling shoes, but is also in the business of high-tech wristbands to monitor athletic performance — something completely different from shoes, but consistent with the rapidly changing and developing technology market. Similarly, Apple has augmented its Core Competency of unique designs and has branched out from computers to add additional creative items that their consumers want, such as phones, iTunes, MP3 players, and other branded products.

Technical Skills

There are two sets of skills in a position description. One set is the Critical Skills and the other set includes the *technical skills*.

Technical skills are those particular skills that, aside from the Critical Skills, are applied on a particular job or function. For example, the technical skills for a corporate treasurer are not the same as those for a vice president of human resources, even though the Critical Skills for each position are the same. Similarly, the technical skills are different from those of a vice president — manufacturing and a vice president — marketing and a partner in a consulting or accounting firm.

An easy way to visualize what technical skills are is to view them graphically as follows:

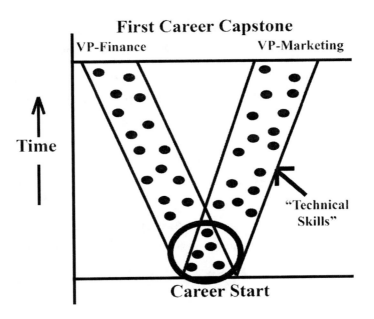

The technical skills to which the arrow points represent the specific skills needed to perform the tasks of a vice president — marketing. As one might suspect, they vary from organization to organization and change over time with developments of technology, reorganization, product change, and the like. In some organizations, these skills might be called "core competencies" that are unique to that particular organization, but I personally hesitate in using the term "core competencies" in describing a job description for an individual. The technical skills are the kinds of skills that, for the most part, are learned within the organization or in similar organizations that market similar products.

Generally when conducting an executive search, the position specification will be written in three parts:

- An overall summary of the position;
- A listing of the specific job tasks and responsibilities; and
- A listing of the skills necessary to be considered as a candidate for the position. The "technical skills" will often be mixed in with the job tasks as well as the listing of skills.

Examples of the technical skills that might be contained in a vice president — consumer marketing position are as follows:

- Demonstrated ability to manage often outsourced marketing activities for consumer packaged goods (public relations, website, etc.)
- Experience in selecting, deploying, and using marketing and sales software applications unique to consumer packaged goods.
- Experience with analyzing and utilizing syndicated research data (e.g. IRI or Nielsen) and primary marketing research (qualitative and quantitative)

These sorts of skills are learned and practiced on the way up the corporate ladder in lower-level positions, and they tend to change over time with advancements in technology or substantive changes in the business. They are the pieces of a mosaic of skills that one builds over time so that he/she will have the necessary qualifications for the first career capstone job. While an individual is busy working in a lower-level position gaining marketing skills, his/her colleague in a financial area is busy gaining skills in the financial function and aiming for the financial first career capstone job.

But technical skills are not the Critical Skills, which are hopefully learned and practiced by **all** who are in the organization . . . and those Critical Skills are a key part of the mosaic for all of the first career capstone positions.

On the Way Up the Corporate Ladder

The key strategy in moving up a corporate ladder is to carefully build a set of skills consistent with those of one of many first career capstone positions. For example, if an individual is interested in a marketing career, he/she might proceed as follows:

Take the first job in the organization in (hopefully) a marketing area. Do as good a job as possible, and concentrate on learning and mastering the Critical Skills as well as those tasks and responsibilities assigned. The first job is shown graphically as follows:

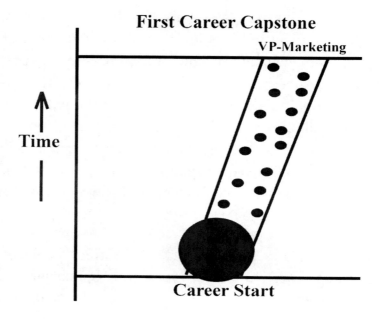

The second job should be within the defined skill mosaic of the target capstone position, regardless of whether the job at the same company where he/she starts.

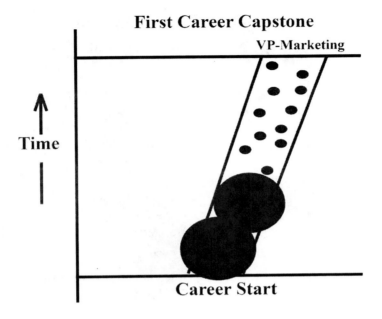

First Career Capstone

Like the second job, the third position should contain techni-cal skills within the target career capstone position as shown below:

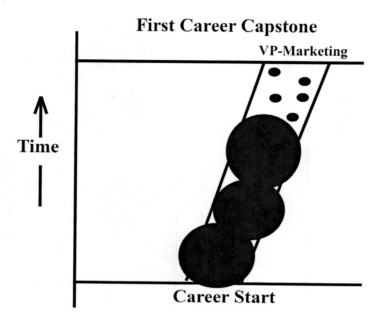

During the course of career advancement and promotion, great care should be taken to keep the skill mosaic as clear and crisp as possible. This advice can also be expressed with the idea that one should not make random or ill-considered lateral moves and blur the skill mosaic.

Roger Nelson, a friend and former Vice Chairman at Ernst & Young, has been a doom loop user both personally and as a manager for over 30 years. His candid advice that mirrors the career capstone skill building strategy is to "climb the mountain of opportunities to learn, and use the doom loop to send you a clear signal when to look for more opportunities consistent with your strategy."

Roger's advice and the career mosaic skill building concept offer an excellent career management strategy. The successive career advancement positions should ultimately enable you to build a clearly defined skill mosaic that should qualify you either for promotion from within or discovery by an external executive recruiter.

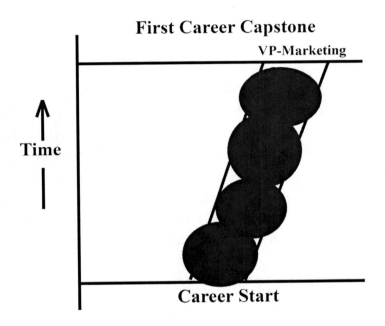

First Career Capstone

On the way up the corporate ladder and throughout a career, the Doom Loop begins to appear in different scenarios and participate in or precipitate various career crises. It is useful in helping you to anticipate various career crises and make short-term or tactical career decisions — **not** strategic decisions. These career crises are discussed in subsequent chapters. The Doom Loop is **not** intended to be a strategic planning tool for career management. That is reserved for the skill mosaic-building process briefly described earlier in this chapter.

Chapter Three

CRISIS #1 – THE FIRST JOB

When you are embarking on some sort of career in any field, there is always that first job following high school or college. The purpose of this chapter is to discuss that first career crisis of what job to take and why.

Generally, some of the things you think about when taking a job for the first time in your career include the following:

- I want to have a job and earn my own money;
- I want to have an apartment and live independently;
- I want to have a car;
- I want to begin my career in a field that interests me;
- I want to live as far away from home as possible.

These are all noble goals, and quite normal. Some individuals spend time preparing detailed career plans and try to find the perfect job that might lead them toward their goals. This, too, is quite normal.

The fact is that it really doesn't matter what job you might take as the first job. Gone are the days when an individual starts work in an organization and spends his/her career without moving to another organization. Another fact is that what you might ultimately have as a career most likely will have no resemblance or connection to that first job, except in one important way: **skills.**

The first job gives you the opportunity to learn and practice the kinds of skills that will be essential for your success in life. Hopefully you have had the foresight to focus on Critical Skills development in high school, college, or graduate school. These skills are generally not the technical skills inherent in a particular organization or field; instead, those skills include the Critical Skills as described in Chapter Two and include:

- Communication
- Production
- Information
- Analytical
- Interpersonal
- Technology
- Time Management
- Continuous Education

Wherever you go after that first job, the Critical Skills that are learned will accompany you. The technical skills that you have learned in the first job may or may not be relevant to future career jobs, but the Critical Skills will certainly have relevance. So you should concentrate on learning and practicing those skills, and that should be your primary strategic goal.

Accordingly, the best advice for you when you are facing that first career crisis is this:

- Throw out all of your criteria that you may have thought of when doing initial career planning with no work experience.

- Take a job with an organization that has a reputation for doing things well. That will ensure that the things you learn in that first job are more likely to be constructive to your career, rather than giving you some negative skill or knowledge baggage to carry with you as you move forward.

- Take a job that will put you somewhere in between Q1 and Q2 on the Doom Loop — that is, you like most of the things you will be doing, and you are good at some and not good at others. This will ensure that you have a spark of motivation to learn as you move forward in that first job.

- Take time to identify first level career capstone positions and determine the kinds of skills and knowledge it will take for you to achieve such a position.

- Do whatever your job requires, at the best of your ability.

- Concentrate on learning and practicing the Critical Skills.

The first job gives you the opportunity to integrate academic learning with workplace know-how and actually put to work what you have learned in school. This may or may not be the first time that you have had such an opportunity, but it is absolutely the best time to begin the application of practical knowledge in the workplace.

The importance of learning and practicing the Critical Skills in the first job cannot be overemphasized, because in two or three years, you will have gained enough experience to achieve some advancement in the organization—**or** you will run into *Career Crisis #2 — First Job Disappointment.*

Chapter Four

CRISIS #2 – FIRST JOB DISAPPOINTMENT

The first job disappointment crisis occurs when you have taken a job in a field which you heretofore thought would be your career of interest, only to discover that you made a mistake. This crisis is a strategic career management glitch in your planning. Typical situations like this happen when you grow up in a family where your mother or father has a career in some field, such as engineering, and, as a child, you want to follow in Mom's/Dad's footsteps. When you are finally in such a job, you find out that they simply don't like it, and quickly find yourself in Q3 or Q4, where feelings of frustration or pure misery abound.

If you go into any MBA classroom at any school, ranging from the very best to the marginal, you will find individuals who are taking the next step after experiencing crisis #2. The students are doing what is called "radical retooling" and preparing themselves for something else in life, as well as augmenting their credentials. The same is true, but to a lesser extent, in other graduate school programs such as law or medicine.

As a typical example, a young man grows up in a household where his father is an electrical engineer. The father is a fine man, one to emulate in life, and seems very happy in what he is doing. The young man observes this and focuses on science in high school, and then goes to the best college he can find and receives a degree in electrical engineering. Then he takes a job with a large electronics company, designing circuit boards. Quickly, he finds that he does not like the work at all, and finds it difficult to be motivated, is frustrated, and on the verge of being unhappy and miserable. In Doom Loop terms, he is somewhere between Q3 and Q4. His solution to the problem is to radically retool, so he leaves the organization and enrolls in the MBA program at a prestigious school.

Other examples include some of my US Naval Academy classmates who, upon graduation, entered the US Navy as officers and during the course of their six-year commitment to the Naval Service, found that a military career was just not what they wanted. Their solution was to either go directly into a job with a corporation or to go to graduate school. The education provided by the military academies enables graduates to go to virtually any graduate school they might choose in nearly any field imaginable. Examples of graduates who have left the naval service include those who are physicians, lawyers, actors, accountants, business executives, professional football or basketball players, members of the clergy, and the like. *This is radical retooling at the extreme.*

Less fortunate examples include professional athletes who experience stardom and accolades through college and enter the world of professional sports, where they immediately enjoy high levels of compensation. In an article by the RAM Financial Group, an organization catering to the professional athlete, the average career spans of professional athletes are as follows:

- National Football League: 3.5 years
- National Basketball Association: 4.8 years
- Major League Baseball: 5.6 years
- National Hockey League: 5.5 years

Most professional athletes find themselves somewhere in the workforce, following a relatively brief professional career. Many make the transition well and become successful in a wide variety of careers: John Mengelt (executive recruiting); Roger Staubach (real estate); Jerry Richardson (fast foods); Terry Bradshaw, Howie Long, Michael Strahan (television broadcasting); Jim Juriga (veterinarian); Michael Jordan (professional sports owner); and the like.

The bottom line in Career Crisis #2-First Job Disappointment-is that after you take a radical retooling step, you will ultimately find yourself back at a career crisis similar to Career Crisis#1- The First Job. The difference this time, however, is that you will (hopefully) face this crisis with stronger Critical Skills and you will probably have a few more street smarts as well as a mountain of debt - but you will most likely start your new job at a higher level of compensation.

After successfully navigating Career Crisis #2 and having settled down in a new and rewarding job with a new company, you can enjoy yourself in Q1 and Q2; for most, however, *Career Crisis #3 — Doomed Before Capstone — is just around the corner.*

Chapter Five

CRISIS #3 — DOOMED BEFORE CAPSTONE

Doomed Before Capstone is the number one career crisis in the American workforce. Remember that the Gallup report said that "71% of the American workforce is frustrated and bored" — and that this seems to occur more frequently among college graduates.

As described in Chapter Two — The Skill Mosaic, there is a threshold level of management — I called it a *first career capstone position* — a position through which you **must** pass in order to advance to upper-level management. Such first career capstone positions includes those in which you are actually in charge of some function or group . . . such as a vice president — finance, or a vice president — marketing, or perhaps a first-level partner in a management consulting, accounting, or law firm. Each career capstone position has a skill mosaic associated with it as shown below for the positions of VP — marketing and VP — finance:

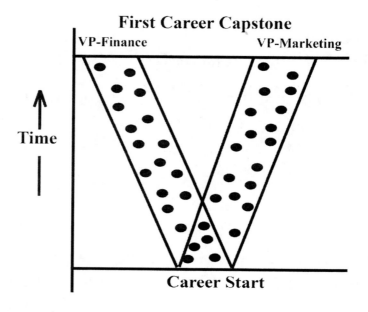

First Career Capstone

VP-Finance   VP-Marketing

Time

Career Start

The recommended career strategy if you want to advance to upper-level management is to build a skill mosaic that looks like one of the first career capstone positions. In these cases, if you are in the marketing area, build a mosaic that looks like a VP — marketing; similarly, if you are in the finance area, build a mosaic that looks like a VP — finance. The concept is simple.

The trouble arises when you are in a position below the capstone level and you have been in that position long enough to move up the curve on the Doom Loop. If you stay in that position for an extended period of time, the cluster of your "good ats" and "likes" will move upward and to the right and pass over the top of the Doom Loop into Q3. When you reach the top of the curve and start entering Q3 from Q2, you are doomed, as shown below:

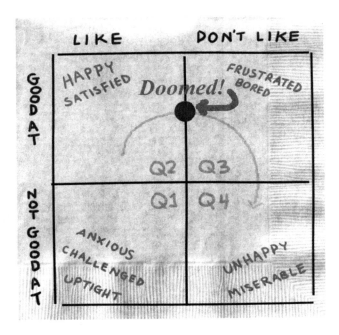

If you stay in that position for a longer time, you run the risk of moving further on the curve and start to drift downward to the dreaded Q4. That's not good. You need to make a tactical decision of some sort to stay focused on your career management strategy.

An interesting feature of the Doom Loop is that you can *actually predict that this movement is going to happen* — sooner or later (if you have the capacity to learn) you will move into Q3. *Count on it.*

An interesting fact about the Doom Loop is that *smarter people tend to rise faster on the learning curve than those who might not be so bright*. While this has its merits — being able to gain competencies quickly — it also has its pitfall. Smarter people tend to become doomed faster than others. It's a fact — and it creates dangerous risks regarding a person's career management strategy.

Not long ago a young man with a Harvard MBA came to me for some career counseling advice. He had received his MBA degree about seven years before we met and he was complaining about frustration and boredom in his job as a marketing manager for a consumer packaged goods company. One of his frustrations was that he was seeing younger people whom he felt were less qualified than he getting promoted in the company while he seemed to be stagnating. I mentally Doom Looped and discovered that he indeed was perhaps overqualified for what he was doing, but also noted that he was working for the third company since receiving his degree. His skill mosaic was a bit blurred. His career management strategy was being compromised by bad decision-making.

It turns out that this young man had eagerly responded to executive recruiters (headhunters) who were seeking individuals for positions lower than the first career capstone. The attractive thing for him was the higher level of compensation that they were offering, so without giving a job change much thought, he switched jobs. Not only did he do this once — *he did it twice.* He fell victim to what I term the *"anesthetic value of compensation,"* and didn't think about the fact that he would be doing essentially the same job with the new company as he was with the other. The anesthetic value of compensation is dangerous, because it makes individuals blind to their strategy (if they have one) of building a sharp and clear skill mosaic. His was becoming blurred, and it was no wonder that individuals who had been in the new organizations longer than he had begun to rise above him.

This is a common occurrence. Very smart individuals are juicy targets for recruiters, and are susceptible to being lured toward jobs that have higher compensation levels but do not add value to their skill mosaic. They make dumb career management tactical decisions. Unfortunately, I have seen a lot of this.

Taking a Job at the Top of a Doom Loop

*Taking a job at the top of a Doom Loop is something you **do not** want to do.* While a higher level of compensation might be attractive in the short term, it is usually a costly penalty to pay in terms of blurring a skill mosaic. It can lead to your being categorized as a "job hopper," and there are a lot of very smart individuals in the corporate world who fall into this category because they made ill-advised career management tactical decisions.

Whenever you are evaluating a potential job — inside or outside of your organization — take a little time and "Doom Loop" the job. Make sure that whatever the job requires you to do has tasks/responsibilities that you like and are good at, **plus** some that you also like but might not be so good at. The job should put you somewhere in a combination of Q1 and Q2. Look at these tasks as opportunities for you to learn. If the job that you are considering might put you at the top of a Doom Loop, do not take it. Stay put — and wait for the right opportunity. Be smart about your career management tactics.

Beware of the Headhunters!

There are two types of executive recruiters: contingency and retainer.

Retainer executive search people get paid regardless of whether you take a job for which they are conducting the recruiting effort. Consequently, they have no real incentive to try to talk you into moving from your organization to another in order to complete the search and get paid for their services. The chances that their sales pitch will be strong are less than if their compensation depended on your making a move.

Contingency recruiters get paid **only if** you take the job for which they are conducting the search. While by far most contingency recruiters are highly ethical, all do have an incentive for you to make a change — their compensation depends on it. Consequently, always ask the recruiter if he/she is retainer or contingency. If contingency, then proceed very cautiously in your evaluation of the job change.

Look Internally First!

Being "doomed before capstone" is a relatively common event, and it happens to almost everyone during one time or another. If it happens to you, do not think that your first move should be to float your resume with the executive search industry. *Look internally first*. Most organizations who value their employees want them to succeed, and most are open to a candid discussion about an employee being a bit bored and frustrated on the job.

So if you find yourself "doomed before capstone," find some-one — perhaps your boss, or perhaps someone in the human resources area — with whom you can have a candid discus-sion. Generally they will be helpful to you and make an attempt to assist you with this common problem. They should be aware that individuals who become "doomed" quickly are generally the brighter ones, and it is much easier to fix the problem inter-nally than to lose a good employee and incur the cost of going outside to recruit someone else.

There are many internal tactical remedies for the "doomed be-fore capstone" individuals. Smart employers will recognize and respect this phenomenon before it happens and will be pre-pared to either promote you or add additional responsibilities that will enable you to move the cluster from Q3 to Q2, or even to a combination of Q2 and Q1 as follows:

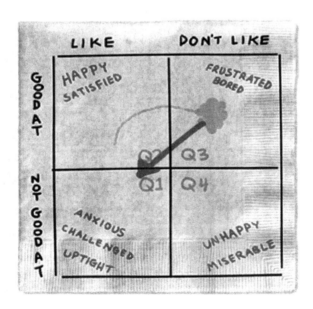

Provided that such an action would add to your skill mosaic and not blur it, this is a much smarter tactic and a better recipe for success than simply ignoring the real frustrations of a good employee. It is an excellent way to recharge your batteries and further motivate you in the organization.

The Preference/Performance Discontinuity

A limitation of the Doom Loop for which you should be aware is the discontinuity between preference and performance. In Doom Loop terms, it is the discontinuity between "like/don't like" and "good at/not good at."

- Understand that **you** are the one who has the feelings and knowledge that you like something or just don't like it.

- Conversely, it is **your employer** who has the knowledge — because of seeing the product of your work — that you are either good at what you are doing or are not good at it.

Therefore, bear in mind that when you do a Doom Loop analysis on yourself, you are measuring your performance from your own perspective — *not from your employer's perspective.*

Likewise, when the employer sees you in your job, he/she is not really aware if you like or dislike what you are doing — that is, unless you tell him/her.

This calls for a healthy dialog between you and your employer. Obviously there are some organizations that are not so receptive to an open and healthy dialog about how you feel about your job and whether you like or don't like what you are doing.

Good employers welcome openness in such communications because it is a healthy thing for the organization. Good employees are hard to find and expensive to lose. Employees who enjoy what they are doing and are motivated and challenged by the requirements of their job are productive and valuable — and are the ones the employers want to keep. Such employers welcome openness and candor in dialog with their employees.

The Four-Month Happy Experience

The four-month happy experience is what you might encounter if you take a job at the top of a Doom Loop.

The simple act of changing jobs — moving from one organization to another, and perhaps from one city to another — can be thrilling and exciting . . . at least for a while; but it can be a dumb tactical career move.

Generally, it takes about four months for you to get accustomed to your new surroundings, your new fellow employees, the different commute you make from home to your job, the different places where you can have lunch with fellow employees, your higher level of compensation, and your new surroundings in the office.

But — if you changed jobs simply because of higher compensation or for some other reason other than to enhance your skill mosaic, after about four months you will most likely find yourself drifting back into Q3 simply because you took a job at the top of the Doom Loop. You will find yourself being frustrated and bored, albeit at a slightly higher standard of living.

In summary, doomed before capstone is the most common and arguably the most dangerous of the seven career crises, mainly because there are so many opportunities to make bad career decisions. So if you find yourself in this particular career crisis, take great care in making any precipitous career decisions, so as to not blur your mosaic.

Think "internal" first — long before you decide to jump ship.

Chapter Six

CRISIS #5 — HAPPY BELOW CAPSTONE, BUT DOOMED!

The Doom Loop was originally created to provide help and guidance for MBA students who were either starting out on a track toward upper-level management positions, or those who had already been on that track for some time. However, suggesting that everyone who has a job aspires to become a chief executive officer is ludicrous! In fact, most people who are employed are not MBA students or top-management achievers, but simply want to have a productive job that provides them with job satisfaction as well as a dependable paycheck so they can lead a happy and comfortable life. Most of the individuals who fall in this category do not even set as a career goal the first capstone position.

So if you are in the very common category of those who do not aspire to reach top management, you are quite normal — but rest assured that the Doom Loop is not ignoring you! And if you are a manager of an organization or department that consists of many employees who are looking for job satisfaction but aren't getting it because of boredom on the job, you should have cause for concern. Boredom has a direct effect on productivity!

The Gallup report pointing out that 71% of the workforce is bored or frustrated on the job did not restrict its sample population to those individuals who have MBA degrees and are fighting their way up the corporate ladder. Far from that, the vast majority of the sample included those individuals with little or no capstone position aspiration.

For this large population of productive employees who do not seek managerial positions for any reason whatsoever, frustration and boredom on the job can be real problems. The remedies for boredom and frustration generally are to get involved with activities that perhaps are not job-related, or to get involved with activities within the organization that require employee participation. The latter of these two remedies calls for an open line of communication between employee and employer. *Employers need to be receptive to discussions about the natural causes of boredom.*

A young woman who is a career medical technician and who enjoys her laboratory work had feelings of frustration and boredom on the job. She had gone into Q3 in a job she wanted to keep. Within her medical clinic, however, there were several committees that encouraged non-management employee participation. She joined a committee that focused on improving patient satisfaction with the clinic, and spent time with others devising ways to make patients who were visiting the clinic more comfortable. In a sense, this was a customer service committee that sought information from patients about their visits by using patient feedback forms where patients could express their level of satisfaction about their clinical visits. From this information, the committee could make recommendations and actually implement programs to address these patients' concerns or suggestions. This participation expanded her work on the job and led to more job satisfaction, and relief of her frustration and boredom.

An example of how an employee can become proactive and creative when faced with boredom on the job is the situation faced by Michelle, who was a mid-level employee in the market research department of a large consumer packaged goods company. Changes in management led to her having a new boss, with whom Michelle felt that she had fallen out of favor. The new responsibilities she was given were beneath her skills and experience, and she began feeling distinctly underutilized.

But far from withdrawing into a glum silence and a frustrated tolerance of the situation, Michelle faced the situation in a proactive way — not lamenting her plight and thinking, "Poor me!" She enthusiastically did her job while quietly drawing attention by seeking greater responsibilities and volunteering to participate in group projects. This positive attitude brought her to the positive attention of her boss who, fortunately, responded by assigning her to two group projects that were slightly unrelated to her job. These new activities and group involvement led to a change in her feelings on the job, essentially moving her from Q3 to Q2, where she began to feel a greater degree of job satisfaction, importance, and self-fulfillment.

Fortunately for Michelle, her boss had the foresight to listen to her concerns and her positive approach to her situation, and responded constructively with the overall organization well-being in mind. She recognized that employee productivity results from a strong level of job satisfaction and took constructive steps toward providing a remedy for Michelle.

Douglas LaBier, a psychologist and the Director of the Center for Progressive Development in Washington, DC wrote a very constructive article about the causes and remedies for boredom in the workplace. This article which appeared in 2010 in the magazine *Psychology Today* is titled *"Feeling Bored at Work? Three Reasons Why and What Can Free You."*

Dr. LaBier provides excellent reasons why boredom on the job occurs, and offers individuals who are experiencing such boredom (i.e., Q3) the following steps, which are quoted directly from his article:

Steps You Can Take To Liberate Yourself

"The first step towards freeing yourself from any of [the various] kinds of boredom is seeing your situation with a clear eye. Step outside of your own narrow vantage point, rather than becoming trapped within it or blocked by feelings of frustration and resentment. When you use '<u>creative indifference</u>' you're better able to [take the next steps and] direct your energy towards finding a better situation. That's the 'creative' part. For example:

- List any situations, jobs, or creative projects from the past where you felt you were at your best, when things went really well. Identify the resources or conditions you had going for you that supported your success. What kinds of people were your co-workers or boss? Did they help or hinder? From that information, identify the specifics of the career and work environment that you really need to be at your best, including which to avoid, and make a list of all of them.

- Scope out any opportunities for more stimulation or greater challenge that you can spot within your present situation or organization. Ask around, or network to find things you may not have noticed yourself. Craft a strategy to pursue them.

- Meet with your boss and explain that you want to take on a greater challenge, or that you want to stretch in a new direction. How do you read his or her response in terms of your future there?

- Seek out an opportunity outside of work, maybe through a course, a seminar or workshop, or a volunteer opportunity, in order to learn something that enhances your existing skills or that builds new ones.

"As you put together all of the above information and feedback, aim towards identifying the kind of work environment, people, organizational culture, or type of work you need that energizes you. List them, and compare them with your present situation. This will help you."

Source: Douglas LaBier, Ph.D., is a psychologist and the Director of the Center for Progressive Development in Washington, DC. *Psychology Today*; May,2010

The simplest, but perhaps the most difficult remedy to address boredom on the job is to become proactive — not fall back into a stupor or negative trance. If becoming proactive in a positive sense does not remedy the situation, then perhaps you should consider either a different line of work, or a different organization more receptive to addressing the normal condition of employee boredom.

Chapter Seven

CRISIS #5 — FIRED

Ouch!

The mere word "fired" brings back memories of yesteryear when that word had a decisive negative stigma. People who were "fired" were among the untouchables.

This chapter focuses on the use of the Doom Loop in cases where an individual is seeking a job after having been let go or fired for some reason. There are many books that describe strategies and tactics about how to proceed when looking for a new job under such circumstances, and if that is what you are seeking, you should consult those books. There are also a plethora of high-quality outplacement firms — firms where you can hang your hat after being fired, and use their resources to assist you in your job search. Whatever you use, however, it is important for you to use the Doom Loop when you consider a new job after being fired.

Being fired isn't so bad these days as it was a generation ago. In fact, being fired is something that many people in virtually any career nowadays might expect to experience.

There are different ways of being fired. One is the simple "You're fired!" for cause, or for some other reason that might be real or trumped-up. Another is being "let go" due to a merger or sale of the business or automation of your function. Still another is "self-firing," which is what I did when I finally realized that I was in Q3 and headed for Q4 in the executive search business.

The executive search profession is a fine one, but the substance of the work is more process-oriented, and I'm more of a creative type. So it was pretty easy for me to become a bit frustrated and bored in that type of work — even though it was very lucrative.

I left the executive search business completely and put myself in Q1 in the world of education and skills. I had no education credentials, but I did know a lot about skills and liked the subject. The trouble was that I had no product to sell to that market and I really didn't have a clue regarding what sort of products and services were needed in the education world.

At this time, the federal government had passed the School to Work (STW) Opportunities Act of 1994 and I quickly became a national STW technical assistance provider. It was clear that there was a significant need for some sort of system that would enable STW coordinators in schools to manage work based learning programs. My solution to this was to develop a STW work-based learning management system called Coop2000® and provide that system to schools and training organizations that had received STW grants. The product was highly successful, reaching over 4000 sites in over 40 states.

Finding myself in Q1 was a highly motivating experience, since I had to create something to meet the needs of those organizations participating in the program. After creating Coop2000®, I quickly moved up into Q2 and enjoyed a few years of highly rewarding times (professionally and economically) until Congress eventually defunded the program. When that occurred, I changed the nature of the system to data collection for special education needs and provided the data collection system for the California WorkAbility program.

The lesson I learned from this experience was that putting yourself in Q1, while risky, can be a terrific motivating event. *It worked for me, and I would do it again.*

When you are fired or let go, there is a lot of pressure on you and your family to find another job and find it quickly. You are caught between the threat of income loss — even though you may have received a substantial severance package — and the stigma of being out of work. The situation of being in between jobs after being fired is highly uncomfortable, and you, like any normal person, want that feeling of discomfort to end as soon as possible. Coupled with the clock ticking away your severance package, the pressure is definitely on to remedy the situation fast.

Saying "No!" When It Hurts

Sometimes after conducting a long job search after being fired, you will be offered a job and the pressure for you to take it will be enormous. You might have to find the courage to say "No!"

The problem is the perception recruiters and employers hiring people have about evaluating candidates. Who is the "best candidate" for a job? Is it the person who is good at everything on the list? Most search committees think so — and a lot of recruiters think so as well.

I disagree.

The candidate who is "good at" everything on the position specification is a candidate who, if he/she takes the job, will most likely be taking a job at the top of a Doom Loop, and *this is something that you don't want to do — except in a dire emergency and with your eyes wide open.*

If you find yourself out of work after having been fired, no matter what the reason, you should be meticulous about evaluating any job opportunity that might come your way. In the "fired situation," the pressure will usually be high to accept some job — any job — and relieve that pressure...be it psychological, financial, or whatever. You must recognize that when recruiters interview you for any reason after you have been fired, they will naturally be far more critical of your qualifications and background — mainly to give them some cover. Employers, too, will be extra cautious and critical of your background when interviewing you after you have been fired. Both the recruiters and employers are human, after all, and they want to make sure that if you have made any mistakes leading to your termination, you will not bring that sort of baggage with you. Accordingly, each will be extra careful to make sure you are "good at" everything on the position specification requirements.

This extra caution taken on the part of the recruiter and employer naturally increases their scrutiny when evaluating candidates, and they want to ensure that any candidate in such a circumstance is "good at everything." In Doom Loop terms, they tend to put a candidate at the top of a Doom Loop, and this is not always wise when seeking a candidate for long-term employment.

Accordingly, if you find yourself being recruited for a job that puts you at the top of a Doom Loop, show the difficult courage to say "No!" to such a job. If you accept such a position, you will be finding yourself — after the four-month get-acquainted time — right back in Q3: frustrated and bored in your new job. So if you do say "Yes!" to such a job, do it with the knowledge that Q3 awaits. Saying "No!" is very difficult under these circumstances, but the alternative is worse if, after four to six months, you decide that the job was not for you and you start making plans for another job change.

Chapter Eight

CRISIS #6 — DOOMED AT CAPSTONE

Alas! When you reach the first career capstone position and even if you have reached positions above first level capstone — including the Chief Executive Officer job — *the Doom Loop will still follow you.*

That is to be expected, because you still have responsibilities and tasks to be performed in whatever job you might hold, and you still have the capacity to learn.

At first level capstone and above, however, the kinds of tactics you can employ change somewhat. You may find yourself having to adjust what you do while still keeping the same job — and this is the preferred tactic.

In such positions at or above first career capstone, you will find yourself an attractive target for executive recruiters who have been engaged to fill positions in other organizations. You will receive many calls from recruiters who will describe what they are searching for and ask you for suggestions, as well as the level of your own interest in making a move.

Here are a couple of examples of doomed at capstone:

The office manager of a medical practice was on the verge of quitting her job. She was extraordinarily good at what she did, but was obviously frustrated and bored in the job. I had a chance to sit and talk with her about the Doom Loop, and she immediately pointed out that she was in Q3. The solution we arrived at was to have her work only three days per week at the same level of pay. She wasn't good at doing her job in a lesser amount of time, and this tactic (with which she agreed) was highly successful. She found herself motivated and happy again, and still is in that role doing a marvelous job.

Another individual was the CEO of a large commodity exchange. He had the habit of coming to work very early in the morning (sometimes at 4:00 a.m.) and by 10:00 a.m. found his work for the day completed. He was frustrated and bored in his job and didn't know what to do. The solution in this case was to get him on the board of directors of a large beer company that was having problems, as well as putting him in an active role as a trustee of a major university. The key here was that he wasn't good at doing all of these things in the amount of time he had available, so the additional roles put him back in the lower part of Q2 and made him very happy. The time compression tactic using the Doom Loop worked.

If you are doomed at capstone, the time compression tactic won't always work; there just may not be any opportunity to expand your responsibilities or role.

If that is the situation, then you might consider alternative organizations and be receptive to executive recruiters.

At the first career capstone position and above, generally the executive recruiters you will encounter are those who are with retainer firms — that is, those firms who are retained for a search and whose compensation is not linked to your accepting a position for which they have been engaged to search.

Even if you are approached by a retainer executive search firm, you would be very wise to look at the position being offered and Doom Loop yourself. You still run the risk of making a lateral move into something that, after the four-month period, you might not find fully satisfying. Make sure that whatever is offered at least moves you to the left into Q2 — but not close to the top of the Doom Loop.

Chapter Nine

CRISIS #7 — RETIREMENT

You have reached the point in your career where you can retire!

Congratulations!

But . . . alas again! The Doom Loop goes with you and doesn't retire at all; in fact, it can rear an ugly side of its personality, so it might be wise to heed its warnings. *The consequences can be fatal.*

Significant evidence points to the fact that retirement — particularly early retirement — can lead to premature death, or, at best, a significant decline in personal health.

In 2005, a study of Shell Oil employees showed that individuals who retire at age 55 and live to be at least 65 die sooner than people who retire at age 65. After age 65, the early retirees have a 37% higher risk of death than their counterparts who retired at 65. Moreover, the study showed that people who retire at age 55 are 89% more likely to die in the 10 years after retirement than those who retire at 65.

This isn't surprising. Most people who are actively engaged in work and have been during a career are not good at doing nothing, and they generally don't like being idle. This is Q4, so it seems obvious that their feelings might lean toward being unhappy and even miserable.

When it comes to happiness and satisfaction in retirement, the key is to keep busy by doing things you enjoy. The real measure of your success can be the quality of life that you build for yourself when you spend your time in retirement.

Many successful people spend more than forty years in their careers. Their lives have been their work: it's been a habit, a part of life, and a daily expectation. Seeing that come to an abrupt end on the day after they retire can be more shocking than a cold shower.

So what can you do about it?

There are two major considerations to think about when planning for retirement.

- Financial security
- Retirement activities

There are many books written about how to plan your finances to ensure that you have a retirement that will be relatively free of financial stress. *This book is not such a financial planning guide.*

There are also many books written about the kinds of activities that one can pursue after retirement. *This is not a book to discuss all of the kinds of things that you can do upon retirement.*

Instead, my counsel to you is to consider the Doom Loop in your planning. Seek out and explore those kinds of things that you like to do, and ensure that in whatever you choose, you are not really "good at" doing such a thing. Don't be afraid to choose something that might put you in Q2 or even Q1. *Just make sure you like what you are doing. The resulting motivational effect of Q1 will guide your feelings.*

As an example, my former partner worked in the executive search field for several decades. He loved the work, but eventually faced retirement. Rather than sit home and do nothing (which he was not good at), he started painting and became an artist. He loved painting and now shows his work at several galleries and has his own studio. He deliberately put himself in Q1 after retirement, and now he is happy and content in Q2.

You can do the same thing. The key is to anticipate that you will be entering a new phase of the Doom Loop — so plan accordingly!

Chapter Ten

RECRUITING WITH THE DOOM LOOP

Yes, the Doom Loop has a place in the recruiting world. In fact, I have used it countless times with considerable effectiveness. The Doom Loop was created during a recruiting session — albeit at the MBA level, as described in Chapter One.

Whenever I was in the process of recruiting someone, whether it was looking at a resume or actually conducting an interview, I would Doom Loop the candidate. I would ask indirect questions and mentally place the individual in the appropriate quadrant on the 2 x 2 Doom Loop matrix. Then I would mentally compare where that individual was on the grid with where he/she would be in the position for which I was conducting a search.

Obviously the mental picture was quite rough, but in nearly all cases it seemed to be accurate, and it told me a lot about the individual, as well as helping me develop a strategy to convince the individual to make a move if, in my judgment, such a move seemed to be in both his/her interest and in that of the client.

I would first try to determine which quadrant he/she was in at the current job. If the quadrant was Q3, then convincing him/

her to make a move would be easier and perhaps in his/her best interest. If the individual was in Q2, then perhaps the move might not be in his/her best interest even though he/she might be qualified for the search I was conducting.

I would then mentally picture where the individual would be in the new job. If the new job would put him/her in Q2 or a combination of Q1/Q2, then making a job change might be a good idea. If the new job were to put him/her in Q3, I would proceed no further.

Using the Doom Loop in such a manner is an excellent way to determine not only if a candidate is qualified for a position, but it gives you tips about what sort of things might motivate the individual to change jobs. It also can tell you if a job change is inappropriate.

If you combine the aspects of the Doom Loop that enable you to connect how a candidate feels in his/her current job and how they might react to the new responsibilities of the job for which you are recruiting, along with knowledge of his/her skill mosaic, you have very solid facts with which you can make a constructive argument. You don't need to tell the candidate that you are Doom Looping him/her . . . you can just use the information that it reveals to you privately in your argument. *It works!*

On the negative side, the Doom Loop can also be used by a recruiter whose compensation is tied to the individual's taking a job that might be inappropriate for his/her skill mosaic. The recruiter can rely on those aspects of the Doom Loop that indicate how a candidate feels in his/her current job. *I feel that this sort of use of the Doom Loop is unethical.*

The "Best Candidate"

Is the "best candidate" the one who is good at all of the parts of the position specification? *Not according to the Doom Loop!*

In recruiting a candidate for nearly any position, the best candidate is generally the one who is good at many of the parts of the specification, but is not so good at others. He/she has room to grow — to learn. In Doom Loop terms, the best candidate is the one who is mostly in Q2 and may even have some parts of his/her skill set that are in Q1. The important characteristic of this candidate is that he/she must be given an opportunity to grow and learn as well. Putting him/her in Q2 or in a combination of Q1 and Q2 ensures that will happen.

Often, recruiting committees demand that the candidate they hire is the one who is good at everything. They don't think much about offering the candidate some room to grow — instead, they hire him/her at the top of a Doom Loop. Sometimes this works — more often, it doesn't.

There are times, however, when the best candidate might actually be the one who is good at everything and at the top of a Doom Loop. That situation is one where the position that is being filled is essential in order to turn around some troubled situation. Other than that, however, my best advice is to seek candidates who are in Q2.

Doom Looping a Candidate

Doom Looping is a verb — it is the process of mentally constructing a Doom Loop for an individual that you are interviewing.

When you do this, you do not describe the Doom Loop to the individual. All you have to do is ask questions about his/her experience to determine the level of competency in various aspects of his/her current job, mixed with questions about how he/she feels about the current position.

When interviewing, you can mix questions that relate to the Doom Loop with other interview questions that can help you assess an individual's Critical Skills. By Critical Skills, I mean the following:

- How well does the candidate express himself verbally?
- What evidence is there that shows how the candidate has actually taken some idea and made it real?
- How does the candidate handle the processing and sorting of information? How does he/she test it for validity?
- How does the individual think? Give him/her a simple problem and then have him/her express verbally how it can be solved. The answer of how to solve the problem is not so important as the process by which the problem is addressed.
- How does the individual use technology to solve a problem?
- How does the individual manage his/her time?

- Have the individual give examples of how he/she works with other people in a team project.
- What is the candidate doing to improve him/herself educationally to keep up with the changes in technology?

Always ask questions that are open-ended and do not require a "yes" or "no" answer. In doing so, and as you ask questions about what the candidate perceives his strengths and weaknesses to be, and what she might like or dislike about her previous job, you can create the mental Doom Loop matrix.

Sometimes, however, you encounter candidates whose qualifications, education, experience, and the like might be questionable.

It is unfortunate that perhaps up to 50% of all resumes contain information that is either misleading or just plain false. In order to flesh out some of these misleading statements or assertions, my former partner used to make a statement and then ask one simple question. He would say, "You know that we will conduct detailed reference checks on you by talking to previous employers and individuals who know you well. That being the case, is there anything that you would like to change on your resume? Are there any skeletons in your closet that you would like to discuss now rather than after they might be uncovered during a reference check?" That proved in many cases to be a very effective technique of rooting out misleading or false statements and preventing severe embarrassment later.

There are some sad facts about statements that individuals seeking jobs put on their resumes. The online tech magazine

Daz©Info had an interesting article by Amit Misra in April 2013 which reported some of this disappointing information:

- 33% of candidates boast about their job description in order to earn higher respect;
- 46% of candidate resumes contain false information;
- 70% of college graduate applicants say they would lie in order to get a job;
- 21% of all resumes contain false information about college degrees;
- 29% of all resumes contain false dates of employment;
- 40% of all applicants report false salary information;
- 33% of all resumes have inflated information about their current jobs;
- 27% of all applicants give false references.
- And, sadly, the list goes on.

Don't these people know that employers check what they have written on their resumes and applications? Apparently some don't.

With today's social media, individuals should understand and expect that smart employers will check Facebook and other media for information about prospective candidates.

There are two cases that I distinctly remember where credentials written on a resume were impressive — one way or another.

In the first instance, I was conducting a search for a vice president of manufacturing for a muffler maker. The lead candidate had written a resume which indicated that he had no college degree, with the exception of an MBA from the University of Michigan. That turned out to be true and was quite impressive. In fact, that he had no undergraduate degree, but a graduate degree instead made him an even more attractive candidate. He had every reason to say on his resume that he had an under-graduate degree, but he told the truth. *He got the job.*

The other case involved a presentation I was giving for the Harvard Business School Club of Chicago. I had asked two oth-er executive search professionals to join me, and each provided a background. One of the individuals from a large prestigious firm indicated that he had an MBA degree from Stanford. That turned out to be false. *Sadly, he lost his job as a result.*

An interesting tactic to employ when interviewing a candidate is to just make a statement about something controversial and then just be silent and see how he/she reacts. An example might be "Some people say that the gap between the wealthy and the poor is growing wider, and this is having a detrimental effect on our economy." Then **silence**.

Ask follow-up questions. Listen to what the candidate says about a question you have asked, and then ask her something about what she said. If you really want to be tough, listen to the answer that she gives, and then ask a question about some-thing she said in her response. Do it again and you will have employed the "Ask the third question" tactic. If she success-fully answers the third question to your satisfaction, you can be pretty sure that she knows what she is talking about.

An excellent interviewer is able to "candle" the individual who is being interviewed. By "candle" I mean it is much like holding a candle behind an egg and being able to see what is inside. Psychiatrists are especially adept at this sort of thing—and you can be too, if you practice your interviewing skills.

The bottom line is that the Doom Loop can be a useful tool for a recruiter in assisting him/her to determine whether or not a career move is appropriate for a candidate. If so, it can help to devise a convincing strategy to encourage the candidate to make a move; if not, it can help explain why such a move might not be in the candidate's best interest. In any event, recruiters should give it a try and see for themselves.

Chapter Eleven

AN EMPLOYER'S USE OF THE DOOM LOOP

Yes, employers can use the Doom Loop! In fact, they can and should use it in two different ways:

- As their own career management tool; and
- To communicate effectively with employees and address issues of boredom and frustration on the job.

Employers have careers, too, and they just might be using the tool to provide a little bit of guidance in their own career management. If this is the case, then the other chapters in this book will apply directly to them.

If, on the other hand, they want to use it with their employees, then that is a healthy sign! It is particularly healthy if employee productivity is a goal.

As described in the introduction of this book, according to the Gallup poll, "Seventy-one percent of American workers are 'not engaged' or 'actively disengaged' in their work, meaning they are emotionally disconnected from their workplaces and are less likely to be productive. That leaves nearly one-third of American workers who are 'engaged,' or involved in and enthusiastic about their work and contributing to their organizations in a positive manner. This trend has remained stable."

The poll also explains that the more highly educated employees tend to be less engaged, and that individuals in the 30- to 64-year-old bracket tend to be less engaged than those who are younger or older. Additionally, the poll found that men tend to be less engaged in their work than women.

That apparently suggests that nearly three quarters of the workforce is in Q3 on the Doom Loop matrix and that both businesses and the US economy as a whole are suffering, with lower productivity than desired. The increased complexity of jobs compounds the problem, because training is expensive and hiring new employees to replace those that leave because of frustration and/or boredom is very costly.

Mr. Fred Mael is an organizational psychologist who does consulting in areas such as talent retention, organizational culture, and performance management, as well as executive and work/life coaching. He wrote an article that clearly articulated the reasons why employers should consider the problem of boredom on the job. This article appeared in the August 2003 issue of *Baltimore SmartCEO* magazine. In the article, he asks the question *"Why Should I Care?"* His relevant comments (quoted directly from his fine article) are as follows:

"A manager or CEO may be inclined to dismiss being bored as a minor annoyance, hardly anything for management to have to attend to. In fact, boredom is seen by many as a boutique emotion of recent vintage and a result of modern society being impatient, overly stimulated, and unrealistic in its demand that work and life always be interesting and meaningful. Unfortunately, that view would ignore the fact that chronic boredom is associated with a host of ills including increased alcohol and drug abuse, excessive smoking, pathological gambling, increased stress-related ailments, alienation from coworkers, and excessive eating and weight gain. Being underemployed, defined as being in a job whose demands are below the person's capabilities, is associated with frustration and discontent, reduced job satisfaction, reduced organizational commitment, and increased job searching behavior.

"It also spills over into negative attitudes towards work and one's career in general, isolation from family and friends, marital tensions, and hampered decision-making ability. You may feel that your employees should be able to grow up, find something productive to do, or try harder. Fine — but you ignore the discontent of these employees (and soon to be ex-employees) and the loss of their expertise, experience, and loyalty at your own peril. Establishing a culture in which people can admit to needing more challenging work without fear of punishments such as being sentenced to busywork is an important first step. Additional steps will have to take the individual, the direction of the company, and the resources you have available into consideration. Leaving the company may be the employee's best recourse — but it shouldn't be the first and only option."

This is wise counsel to all employers.

The remedy for treating boredom is for managers to do something to relieve it, but what can be done is difficult to understand, and perhaps harder to actually do.

The most obvious first step is to recognize the fact that boredom and frustration exist in the workplace, and are quite normal phenomena. If this is recognized by managers, then the next step is to encourage employees to talk about it openly with their managers — after all, each has the same goal of relieving the boredom — about how the employees can obtain more job satisfaction and the employers achieve higher productivity.

The scholarly study *"The Unengaged Mind: Defining Boredom in Terms of Attention"* by Eastwood, Frischen, Fenske, and Smilek, defines boredom as "the aversive state that occurs when we:

- are not able to successfully engage attention with internal (e.g., thoughts or feelings) or external (e.g., environmental stimuli) information required for participating in satisfying activity;

- are aware of the fact that we are not able to engage attention and participate in satisfying activity, which can take the form of either awareness of a high degree of mental effort expended in an attempt to engage with the task at hand or awareness of engagement with task-unrelated concerns (e.g., mind wandering); and

- attribute the cause of our aversive state to the environment (e.g., "this task is boring," "there is nothing to do").

This appears to mean that employees generally have low attention spans because of activities that are not satisfying, and they attribute this to their workplace or environment. The study also suggests that boredom leads to less than optimum performance on the job.

What are the remedies to relieve boredom in the workplace? A review of many studies on the subject of boredom reveals two major efforts that managers can make:

- Develop ways to communicate to employees that their work is valued;

- Encourage openness in communications between employees and management about boredom on the job. The Doom Loop is normal and should be expected to have its effects on all.

Other than these two suggestions, the studies reveal little else of consequence.

On balance, managers not only have to deal with their own personal Doom Loops, but those of their employees as well. The Doom Loop affects all, and the consequences of not paying attention to the needs of employees when they go into Q3 can have quite a negative and unprofitable effect on the entire organization.

Chapter Twelve

OTHER INTERPRETATIONS OF THE DOOM LOOP

The Doom Loop has been around for a while, since I created the little tool back in the late 1970s.

Since that time, others have used it and some have written articles or extensive blog posts about it. I think some of these are excellent interpretations and would like to include them in this chapter.

1) *The Doom Loop System* (book)

I appreciate Dr. Hollander's completion of the book about the Doom Loop. She was introduced to the Doom Loop at a national convention of the American Psychological Association in Los Angeles by me, and expressed interest. After I had obtained an agent and a publisher, I invited her to participate as a co-author because of her excellent credentials and her high level of interest.

I was disappointed with the book, however, because the publisher wrongly thought that the Doom Loop was much more than it really is. Instead of writing a short book about the Doom Loop and putting into perspective that it is constrained by its use of only two variables (preference and performance) and, as a whole, is only a rough guide at best to assist an individual in making tactical career decisions, she went along with the publisher and tried to make this simple little tool a complete "system" of career management. It is not that at all. For example, the book discusses office politics . . . office politics have nothing to do with the Doom Loop. Such additions seemed to me to be just "filler."

Nevertheless, she followed my outline in general when describing the tool, and assisted in popularizing the concept through publication of the book. For that, I am grateful to her and for her efforts.

2) Executive Roundtable

The first article appears in The Executive Roundtable Blog and was written by Glain Roberts-McCabe, the Executive Roundtable founder and president. The Executive Roundtable offers a variety of coaching and mentoring-based programs designed to equip mid-career leaders with the immediate tools, strategies, and insights they need to excel in the near term, and the lifelong mindsets they need to maintain momentum and continue their career success.

The article is titled "The Career Doom Loop Revisited: Are You on a Slippery Slope?" Glain provides a quick and crisp description of the Doom Loop without fanfare or diagrams. This article can be read in its entirety at the following website: http://www.theexecutiveroundtable.ca/are-you-doom-looping-it/

The Career Doom Loop Revisited:
are you on a slippery slope?

March 12, 2012

I've been having lots of career discussions with members recently, so thought I'd revisit this post from 2009. Enjoy. Years ago I was introduced to this great model called "The Career Doom Loop." The concept was created by Charles Jett and popularized in Dory Hollander's book, "The Doom Loop System." It's a simple model that stuck in my head and made my own career path make so much more sense. It goes like this:

When you first start a new position, you are in Stage 1 of the Doom Loop. You are:

in a job you LIKE/that you're NOT GOOD at (goes to reason... when you start out, you don't even know where the photocopier is, never mind how to contribute to your best ability).

Which then leads us to Stage 2. You are:

in a job you LIKE/that you are GOOD AT (you've hit your stride, your contributing, your employer adores you)

Which then leads to the next stage and the time when the Doom Looping begins. You are:

in a job you DON'T like/that you are GOOD AT (ah yes, the boredom factor has kicked in. You're still good, but you're starting to check out.)

Which is when one of two things will usually happen:

1) You continue to slide to the final stage of the Doom Loop: **you don't like your job, you're no longer good at it.** You've probably seen this around organizations. It's often called "dead wood."

or,

2) If you are a high performing fast tracker, **you'll never even hit the fourth and final stage.** You will likely pop yourself out of your organization and head to greener pastures where you can begin again at Stage One in a job you like, but that you're not great at yet.

And there, my friends, lies the lesson. If you are currently managing a fast tracker, **don't stick your head in the sand when you see the boredom factor setting in.** To keep these ambitious types engaged, you have to throw them into a situation that they're excited about but not good at yet. Yes, this might mean transferring them to another department to get a new set of experiences, and that means you're going to have to deal with a hole on your team...but really, isn't that better than them walking out the door and taking all their IP to your competitor?

And, if you are said "fast tracker," here's the thing to think about. If you're working for a boss who hasn't read your boredom and/or doesn't have the wherewithal to issue a new challenge, why not try suggesting one to them yourself? After all, the grass always looks greener when you're getting stuck in a career rut. But sometimes, our best opportunities can be found right under our noses, if we're just willing to look.

Happy leading!

3) SparkpilotBlog

According to the SparkpilotBlog website, the SparkpilotBlog presents "topics relevant to managers or people looking to grow their management, leadership and life skills." An interpretation of the Doom Loop may be found at the following website: (http://sparkpilot.com/blog/?p=189) in a posting entitled *"The Doom Loop System."*

This article, written in December, 2010 by Gavin McMurdo, describes the Doom Loop but wrongly attributes its origin. McMurdo uses his own graphics and attempts to show different perspectives — outsiders and insiders — and offers an online assessment (http://sparkpilot.com/doomloop/) to assist the reader in determining his/her own position in the matrix. To me, this is a creative way to approach the quantification of the Doom Loop, but I personally do not believe that it is necessary. I applaud Mr. McMurdo, however, for attempting to expand the usefulness of the Doom Loop.

4) Keenan MBA Career Resource Center

Mr. John R. Bertrand, Senior Associate Director - EMBA/ GEMBA/One-Year Masters/Alumni Services & Engagement, Keenan MBA Career Resource Center at the Marshall School of Business, University of Southern California published an article titled "Darwin, The Doom Loop, Dreams, and Direction: What Does It Mean to Manage Your Career Today?" This article first appeared in the Spring '08 issue of the *USC Marshall Alumni Career Newsletter.*

Bertrand presents the Doom Loop tangentially and with an entirely different graphic description, but with essentially the same theme. His excellent article provides a variation of the Doom Loop and provides a "Success Loop" as a remedy. He does not describe the Doom Loop in the traditional way it was introduced, but you can quickly grasp the idea, and his creative insight into the Success Loop remedy is helpful.

5) Computerworld

In March, 2004, Mary Ann Wagner and Marguerete Luter wrote a short article in Computerworld titled "Avoiding the Career Doom Loop." This article may be read at the following website address: (http://www.computerworld.com/s/article/90747/Avoiding_ the_Career_Doom_Loop)

The authors describe the Doom Loop as "a term that describes the unfortunate position employees may find themselves in when they are no longer considered important to their company." While this is not my own interpretation of the career management tool that I created, I applaud the authors for using it to help others.

In summary, it is encouraging that others are using the Doom Loop concept to counsel individuals on the management of their careers. Feel free to check out these interpretations and, if they increase your understanding of the concept, *then that is a good thing.*

Personally I think that the Doom Loop is very intuitive and needs no workshops, exercises, or extended training time for explanation. Trying to quantify your "likes" and "dislikes" or your "good ats" or "not good ats" is a waste of time. *The Doom Loop is an intuitive visualization of the results of a differential equation done mentally with qualitative information and needs no further analysis to be useful.*

Chapter Thirteen

REFLECTIONS

Almost 35 years have passed since I interviewed the Harvard Business School student and convinced him not to go into the management consulting field — and the Doom Loop jumped right out of the cocktail napkin at me. With Dr. Barrie S. Greiff's suggestion that I make the device dynamic, the tool was born.

Since that time I have used literally thousands of cocktail napkins explaining the Doom Loop to others. It has been fun, and the tool has been very useful for many.

Some say that the tool is obvious — too simple — and toss other criticisms at it. That's fine, but what they don't know is that it is built on some pretty solid mathematical principles.

Without getting too technical, you can imagine that each human being can be represented by a mathematical equation. That person is a function of literally thousands of variables such as height, weight, gender, etc. Two of the variables include what he or she is "good at" or "not good at" (performance) and whether he or she "likes or doesn't like" (preference) the job tasks.

Mathematically, you can hold all of the other variables in a person's life constant for a period of time and look at just look at preference and performance. You can see how they plot in the matrix over time, and, other variables being held constant, the Doom Loop emerges. That is akin to the application of partial differential equations — *but with qualitative data.*

Of course it is silly to imagine that in all cases the other variables will remain constant over the course of a job. Suppose, for example, that when a person takes a job with a company in a city, the atmosphere in the city is crystal clear. Two years later while the person is in the same job, smog has enveloped the city and makes breathing unbearable. In an instance such as this, the Doom Loop analysis is moot, because the person wants to move out of an untenable environment.

The Doom Loop also ignores how an employee feels about his/her colleagues or his/her boss. If she has a terrible boss, then no matter where she might be on the Doom Loop regarding her job, staying in the job is unbearable and the Doom Loop analysis is again moot.

*So **of course** the Doom Loop has its limitations, but understanding those limitations makes the tool useful.*

With respect to organizations as a whole, I'm not sure if there is an organizational Doom Loop. I know that the term has been used in Europe and elsewhere to describe a particular business or financial condition of a company, but that is not the context to which I'm referring. I have a feeling that there could be an organizational Doom Loop, but have not taken the time or incurred the expense of doing any research to find out. Whether there is or there isn't will be the subject of some future graduate student's Ph.D. thesis, I'm sure.

I have used the Doom Loop on a wide variety of individuals in virtually all industries and all ages. I have used it to counsel high school students about which elective course to take, and I have used it with university presidents about a job change. It doesn't really matter: the Doom Loop appears to apply to all.

The fact that it is not a "loop" per se has never been an issue. To this date I have never had anyone point out that fact to me. Instead, when I describe the little tool to someone, they immediately grasp it and personalize it . . . "I'm right there on the Doom Loop in my job," he will say when pointing to one of the four quadrants. That always seems to happen. *Try it and see for yourself!*

I have always had fun presenting the Doom Loop. Generally I present the concept after discussing the Critical Skills, which are discussed in depth in another of my books called *"WANTED: Eight Critical Skills You Need To Succeed!"* I will explain the skill mosaics, show the Critical Skills, and then jump into the dynamics of the Doom Loop. While to me the Critical Skills are more important in the long run, audience interest generally focuses on the Doom Loop — I suppose because it is very personal.

I have been amazed over the years at the tenacity of the Doom Loop to remain relevant. Currently there appears to be a bundle of research being conducted about boredom in the workplace.

One of these days some researcher is going to discover the Doom Loop, describe it in academic or scholarly terms, call it something else, and claim that he/she discovered something new. That's the way it goes.

In closing, I want to remind you that the Doom Loop is not a "career management system" to help you with your strategic career management decisions. It is a "tactical tool" — a tool that can help you avoid dumb career decisions and a tool that can enable you to recognize an opportunity to grow and learn consistent with your career management strategy. *Don't forget this. The Doom Loop is a tactical career management tool.*

If the Doom Loop helps you to avoid making an ill-advised job change or in any way keeps you from not blurring your career skill mosaic, then I consider this to be "mission accomplished!"

I wish you the very best of luck in your career, and if you have read this entire book, you can consider yourself to be a *Certified Doom Looper!*

Charles Cranston Jett
Chicago, IL
December 2014

CPSIA information can be obtained
at www.ICGtesting.com
Printed in the USA
FFOW01n0047291214
9885FF